SARDINES

Romina Ramos

BENT KEY

Publishing

First published in Great Britain by Bent Key Publishing, 2022
Copyright © Romina Ramos, 2022
The moral right of the author has been asserted.

Northern Dialect was first published in *Ey Up: an Anthology of Northern Poetry*.
2022, Bent Key Publishing.

Photographs © Romina Ramos.

ISBN: 978-1-915320-15-5

Bent Key Publishing
Owley Wood Road, Weaverham
bentkeypublishing.co.uk

Edited by Rebecca Kenny @ Bent Key
Cover art © Samantha Sanderson-Marshall @ SMASH Design and Illustration
smashdesigns.co.uk

Printed in the UK by Mixam UK Ltd.

To my mother, I'm sorry I was such a slippery fish growing up.

To my grandmother, thank you for teaching me how to take the guts from something and keep them for myself.

To my brothers, a pack of sardines is called a family; you are my pack.

Romina Ramos' poems paint with a full palette while maintaining a disarming clarity. Moving between a Portuguese heritage and home in the North West of England, this is writing both evocative and direct, warm yet wryly observant. Difficult themes of dislocation, belonging, and working-class identity are explored with lyrical precision and a light, sometimes humorous touch. Whether they kick like a first shot of *Aguardente* or comfort us like *pão doce* fresh from the oven, these are poems that linger in the memory.

Ben Wilkinson, Writer and Educator

Contents

i

In Line at Sou's   11
On hearing Portuguese spoken in the street   12
Bargain Hunting in the *Best Buy* Aisle   13
Sardines   14
Yeah, but where from *really*?   15
Tradition   16
How Do You Say   17
Northern Dialect   18
My Shoes Are Talking   19
Habitat   20
The Smoker : *after Fernando Pessoa*   21
Iberian Coast   22

ii

Dear Ma / Mãe   24
My Father Was an Athlete / O Meu Pai o Atleta   26
Three Hail Marys and an Our Father / Três Ave Marias e 28
   um Pai Nosso
Snail Picking Before Dawn / Apanhar Caracóis Ao   30
   Amanhecer

iii

Becoming   35
Aguardente   36
Things I Learned in a Previous Life   37
Portrait of notebook as operating theatre : *after Ocean* 38
   Vuong's Dear T

What the seagull said to the sardine   39

Prayer   40

Grey Area   41

Line Cook   42

First Time at the English Seaside   43

Little River Fish   44

To My Future Sardines   45

Acknowledgements / About the Author   47

About Bent Key   52

SARDINES

In Line at Sou's

And the bald guy in the middle
makes a wise crack about my queueing
the wrong way, *the European way*,
he says, *you're in the wrong place, love.*

He stands centre-stage, taking over the tiny
shop floor like he's speaking on a podium.
But he's right. I don't belong on this side of
the road, like him; we're classed differently.

I don't take offence; I tell him that
I voted remain. And we wait. The bulb
flickers, as if to the beat of a heart skipping
and a red moon casts a shadow over the shop.

I guess I have always known, since the first time
I sank my teeth into this anaemic watermelon
and this language dripped sour from my mouth,
that we do things a little differently back home.

People here can be a little tasteless.
And you just know that he is the type of tourist
that goes abroad and spends the first day mapping
out the English breakfasts and Irish pubs

yet misses the irony of calling out
thank you, Boss as he collects his
battered sausage wrapped in old news
and drives off in his Citroën.

On hearing Portuguese spoken in the street

Imagine my ecstasy, my friend, when I hear
our mother drip from your tongue like *Fado*.

The fragrant fried onions of Market Street
are no more, instead you smell like espresso

and *Rua das Lojas*. I want to greet you the proper
way, a kiss on each cheek, invite you to sit

and huddle over a pot of swimming snails.
Tell me about your grandmother's *feijoada*

as we dive, sourdough first, into this memory lane
of flavour. I'm sorry, I know it can be overbearing

but I have been away so long, I will take
a concrete puddle and call it a beach.

Bargain Hunting in the *Best Buy* Aisle

Growing up, we never had the same cereal
twice. There was always food at home,
but we were hungry for security.

We stopped praying before meals, started
begging for survival. I'd swap my dinner ticket
for three Lambert & Butler, sell one back

and make enough to buy bread. And you
knew, when you heard mum's keys in the door
that if you forgot to defrost the chicken

you'd be eating Happy Shopper tins for dinner.
We would go bargain hunting in the *Best Buy*
aisles of this shady town, empty baby pram

trailing behind us, ready to carry home our
bread and butter, hungry baby swinging at the hip
limbs soft like pão doce fresh out of the oven.

Sardines

We were always two or three
to a bed, sometimes nine or ten
to a house, an uncle kipping in the tub.

A school of infants to a pearly cot,
one kitchen for two mothers, a single
pot to feed a dozen mouths.

Though we only ate from tins
and were packed in tight like a
family of sardines, we were happy.

Yeah, but where from *really*?

I come from a place where people drink
eight espressos a day. Where sardines are
fished from the sea at five am and grilled
for tourists at a local restaurant, by noon.

I come from grainy sand and the Atlantic ocean.
I come from long, hot summer days swimming
with inflatable dolphins, and wintery Sunday
mornings building sandcastles with pink gloves on.

I come from Catholic women and faithless
men; I come from women who raise the
children of other women and men who do
not raise their own. I come from single parents.

I came to a place where it rains torrentially
in July, while brightly-coloured trucks whistle
through photocopied streets selling
rainbows and sprinkles to local children.

I came to a place where football is a religion,
fish and chips on a Friday night a tradition, where
schools have uniforms but I am still the odd one out —
plaid skirts can't hide the stretch marks of nationality.

They say *yeah, but where from really?* Like
my split tongue doesn't fit in this island's mouth —
but the thing is, I don't even like sardines, and
I take my coffee white with milk and sugar.

Tradition

We survived the explosion,
crawled through the rubble,
made a sling from threads
of a broken life and flew here
strapped to our mother's back.

Her tongue, a road map to another
mouth. Her feet, paddles as we
crossed seas. Her hands built us
a new life out of old family
traditions sewn together, out of

my grandmother's backbone, out of
translated love and sardine skin.
The walls were whitewashed with
the faded pigment of our skin but we
planted olive branches in the garden.

How Do You Say

I learned English sitting cross-legged
on the cold, creaky floorboards of a council
house, by writing down the lyrics to

Dido's *White Flag* and Sugababes'
Hole in the Head which is fitting because
that's how it felt to lose my own tongue.

The kids next door wanted to play
with me but only to ask how to say
dirty skin in Portuguese. I'd look to

the sun: *home*, I'd say. I came from
the sun, my friends were the waves.
Friends? I'd ask. They would laugh.

How do you say *storm* where you
came from? I learned to say *I surrender*,
in English, soon after that.

Northern Dialect

I cried real gravy tears the first time
someone told me my accent was
thicker than my eyebrows.

I don't understand these Northern insults.

I thought I could speak English until
I moved to Lancashire, where people
eat *tea* and swallow their Ts.

I don't understand this Northern cuisine.

Where I grew up, our fish came straight
from the dock the second it was caught,
not swimming in yesterday's headlines.

I don't understand these Northern sea tides.

I've been paddling upstream,
trying to stay afloat; I've even diluted
my name to fit in your mouth just so —

Yet I still don't understand this Northern diet.

I've eaten nothing but battered sly digs
and back handed mushy peas for two decades:
not you though, you're okay.

My Shoes Are Talking

The holes in my shoes tell a story;
   their previous owner tied a knot
in their throat and threw them up
   to the phone lines on our estate,

where dreams are sold, weighed
   on grandmothers' baking scales, flung
tenner a gram, from the sandwich
   bags of sleepy council estates.

My own grandmother calls the phone
   box on a calling card, I open my
mouth but only sand comes out. I have
   forgotten how to breathe in a

language that she understands. I sing
   to her about a fine summer rain
she can only dream of, while she guts
   sardines under the grilling sun.

Does it burn when you miss us?

Habitat

There is no kitchen on the earth
like my grandmother's. The smell
of sardines grilling just isn't the same
on a brand-new George Foreman.

I have grown gardens in fifth-floor
apartments; you'd be surprised what you
can do when you have no choice but
to become soil yourself. When I say

garden, I mean a glass of water, half full,
my heart stuck between two toothpicks
like an avocado stone desperate to
grow roots. Maybe what I need is not

a house but a place to lay eggs.
Let's call it a coop, or a cave, maybe
a burrow of sorts; I was born in the
wild. I am happy among the earth.

The Smoker
after Fernando Pessoa

I too pluck the souls of flowers
and call myself a gardener.
Is it still mine if I steal it?

I once stole a kiss from a bottle,
sank my teeth into its neck, made
a trench in the glass. I was ready for war.

O Lisbon, my mother, birthed me
then spat me out in a veil of fumes.
I am comfortable in my disquiet.

It is not the river Arade that I love
but the town that carries it on its back
like a mule on market days.

O South, my beloved, I have been
fishing sardines in your salty waters
since your coast gave me permission.

Take my cigarette butt for what it is:
a small campfire, a rescue mission; tell
mother I am lost, but looking for smoke.

Iberian Coast

There is nothing but Mesozoic limestone
and emerald spume for miles, playing on a loop.

The cliffs here have made fortresses of themselves,
holding small beaches in their wombs like secret children.

If you're lucky, you might find yourself swallowed
whole by the watering mouth of a sea cave.

The Iberian coast has a way of enamouring you
with its eyes, lighthouse beams luring you home.

There is something in the way the waves sing;
my feet submerged in water become anchors

I cannot leave. Nor do I want to anymore.
I have made peace with my place at sea.

Dear Ma
after Anabela Vardy

You once wrote that I am like a chair:
not comfortable, but strong and supportive.

If I am so it is because you taught me
to build my own seat instead of waiting

for an invite, it is because you are
the table our family eats at every night.

Your oak limbs have dished out more
difficult discussions than traditional cuisine

and your back has prepared us for wars
we were never going to win, and yet

we stand, unabashed, mother and daughter
table and chair, feeding, holding, there.

Mãe
para Anabela Valério

A minha mãe deu à luz uma metáfora
e batizou-me Cadeira de Madeira.

Desde criança ensinou-me a construir um lugar
a mesa, em vez de esperar que me convidem a sentar.

A minha mãe é uma mesa de carvalho
de onde uma família inteira se alimenta diariamente.

Desde criança ensinou-me a comer
de tal maneira que só sobra a espinha, limpa.

A minha mãe ensinou-me a lutar em guerras
que nunca iriamos ganhar, e ainda aqui estamos

imbatíveis, mãe e filha, mesa e cadeira
alimentando, suportando, amando.

My Father Was an Athlete
for Francisco Ramos

He ran out of the maternity ward so fast
he got to the finish line before I even
opened my eyes for the first time.

Every man that came after him
treated us like it was a race but the
loser was always my mother.

My therapist says this metaphor is
not healthy. But the thing is — my father
was an athlete, he played

professional football for a small
division Portuguese team, so maybe
my mother was the pitch, and I was a

goal in the back of the wrong net.
Maybe instead of a hat-trick I was
a foul, a red card, a stretcher at

half-time. I don't really know much
about football, or about parenthood.
But either way, my father was offside.

O Meu Pai o Atleta
para Francisco Ramos

Saiu do bloco de maternidade
com tanta rapidez que chegou a etapa final
antes de eu abrir os olhos pela primeira vez.

E os homens que chegaram depois
trataram-nos como se fossemos uma corrida
e quem perdia era sempre a minha mãe.

O meu psicólogo diz que esta metáfora
não é saudável, mas o meu pai foi um atleta
que jogou futebol na segunda divisão

e fez da minha mãe relva pisada.
Eu fui apenas um golo na baliza errada
um cartão vermelho antes do intervalo.

Não sou mãe, nem sei nada sobre
futebol, mas de uma coisa tenho certeza
absoluta, o meu pai está fora de jogo.

Three Hail Marys and an Our Father

after Grandma

My grandmother bought me rosary beads from
the Basilica in Fatima, blessed by the Pope himself.

My grandmother, who called my sexuality *a phase*
and lit candles in prayer for my salvation, ay Jesus.

Who loved me unconditionally, under one condition.
I must confess: I am a sinner. I pray to a god that

I don't believe in when I want things the Bible says
I cannot have, like the love of a woman, or when

I don't want the things it says I must, like children.
It's funny, in my darkest days those red, shining beads

are the only light around. When my heart is
so heavy that I cannot get out of bed, those beads

look on with the kindness of my grandmother's eyes.
I often wonder if he knew what I ask of his god,

would Pope Francis still have blessed those beads
or would he have prescribed my penance?

Três Ave Marias e um Pai Nosso
para Avó

A minha avó ofereceu-me um terço
abençoado pelo Papa na Basílica de Fátima.

A minha avó que proclamou a minha sexualidade
uma 'fase' e acendeu velas pela minha salvação. Aí Jesus.

A minha avó que me amava incondicionalmente, com uma
    condição.
Tenho que confessar que sou pecadora. Rezo a um deus

em que não acredito quando quero coisas que a Bíblia
não permite, como o amor de uma mulher

ou quando não quero coisas em que a Bíblia insiste
como filhos. É engraçado então, que nos dias mais escuros

esse terço ilumina-me a casa com o brilho dos olhos
da minha avó. Às vezes pergunto-me se o Papa Francis

soubesse o que eu peço do seu deus, teria ele
abençoado o meu terso, ou absolvido os meus pecados?

Snail Picking Before Dawn
after Grandad

You were a brown bear with
greying fur and I was still a cub
afraid to step out of your shadow.

Your paws were too stern
for the tall grass leaves
but mine were not yet so.

This is why you brought me.
Not because you wanted to
teach me, but because I

didn't need teaching. I could
carry buckets balanced on
my molars back to camp

twice as fast, even with snails
tickling my whiskers. All this
before the cock had sung.

Apanhar Caracóis Ao Amanhecer
para avô

Tu eras um urso grande
de pelo branco, eu era uma ursinha
com medo de sair da tua sombra.

As tuas patas muito brutas
para os fios da relva dourada
as minhas ainda delicadas.

Era por isso que me levavas contigo.
Não porque me querias ensinar
mas porque não era preciso.

Eu carregava baldes cheios, balançados
nos molares os caracóis a coçar
o bigode, tudo isso antes do galo cantar.

iii

Becoming

I was born in a town
turned city, turned water-
well, turned mirage.

Where we hunted
in sea-dunes turned riverbeds,
turned ocean songs.

Where we ate from the water
and drank from the tongues
of mother mountains.

Where women turned
into fish-filleting knives,
into ironed striped ties,

into church offerings.
Young ladies grew and turned
into vessels, into substance,

into misuse. I was born
from sand turned salt,
turned fluid thing.

Aguardente

I did my first shot when I was 7 years old,
damp forehead, eyes wider than the bottleneck.

What is more deceptive than a glass of fire
that looks like water? Can you ever really

trust anything again when the thing that
is meant to hose down your tiny, burning

euphoria, makes of you a volcanic body?
Some lessons are learned before we are taught

to know ourselves. I learned to trust my taste
over my sight; you can never tell how acidic

a person can be simply by looking. *Agua
ardente* translates, literally, to *water burning*.

I have come to realise that I am both
swimming in it and setting it alight.

Thing I Learned in a Previous Life

How to fold a tea towel just so
it resembles a lovely roast chicken.

How to spatchcock it, roll it into
a chorizo and flick it, so fast

you don't see it, so hard it leaves a bruise.
That you never screw the crew

because when the ship sinks and you
jump overboard, the captain will save

every man but you. That although
the walk-in freezer is soundproof

your rebounding shouts will awaken
the frozen carcasses around you.

That only those with leather skin
survive the heat, and I stretched

myself so thin it now flakes
at the sight of a hob. That it takes

a sharper knife to hang up an apron
than to keep on slicing rotting flesh.

That sometimes it takes one existence
to end for a life to truly begin.

Portrait of notebook as operating theatre
after Ocean Vuong's Dear T

Maybe I became a poet to keep you
alive; let's call this pen a scalpel
and these blue latex hands calm.

I have made myself a surgeon
to doctor that last summer and
instead of driving, we flew over.

Some days the pen won't sharpen
and you always die too soon.
I have written you back to life

more times than my eyes can bear.
I am so tired I do not notice your blood
is squid ink, I do not notice until

it is too late, until your arms
are a tangled mess of dying suckers.
You always slip away to the depths.

What the seagull said to the sardine

I can see how your fate might lead
you here, to this deserted dinner plate

with nothing but a chunk of soda bread
to lie on, lemon the wettest thing around.

But how dire must things be for me
to end up here, perched on a metallic

fence outside a brick window, in
a landlocked town, circulating

Biffa bins of chip shops for scraps?!
In another world we would be enemies

but in this life, we have ended up
paddling in the same rocking boat.

Prayer

The town sits below the church
the people above the river
everyone prays but not everybody
fishes, not everybody eats.

There is enough to go around
but it doesn't come cheap
it's a soul for an eye around here
if you feed from the streets.

But the people are rich
if you know where to look
there's gold to be had in these slums
if you know how to cook

from the earth at the bottom
of our feet, there are things
to be grown if you beg for the seed.
Take the flowers from the weeds.

The town cracks below the church
the people clamber to the tower
but there is only silence to be heard
from those with boat and paddle.

Grey Area

Not quite Portuguese
since migrating overseas;
we're a different kind of sardine.

Not quite Hispanic
more like a *bruja*; can't call me
they, but they call me *puta*.

Not quite British
honorary at best, and it's taken
two decades to earn that crest.

Not quite this, not quite
that; have you never seen
a green olive grow from a white flag?

Not quite a boy, not quite
a girl, just a chameleon
in a beige, binary cage.

Not quite brave but not
afraid, not quite religious
but I find myself praying.

Not quite a sinner, not quite
a saint, just too much rainbow
for this Purgatory Grey.

Line Cook

I was almost a chef once.
Spent ten years on the line,
only moved up one rank.

I did the job without the title.
Does that make me the bait
or the boat? Net or shoal?

I almost had my own kitchen
but the heat was too much
even for my hot Iberian blood.

I was almost the best,
the epitome of a *fine dine*
until I became a fine line myself.

I carried the crew to shore
until I became a thread
as frail as whitebait bones.

I almost made it unscathed
but they were slippery things
and never made it to the surface.

First Time at the English Seaside

Even the quicksand
looks at us a little funny.
It doesn't swallow us whole
like one of its own, rather
cakes our feet in muddy disdain.

It has been weeks now
since we've walked through
scorching, loose grains
to reach that foaming mouth,
so we trudge forward

hoping for some of the same.
You would think
my oily skin would adapt well
to these greasy waters,
but it flakes and loses scales.

Little River Fish

We thought swimming in these waters
meant we owned them, learning

along the current that our bodies
were not our own to take just anywhere.

Some tended to their young the only way
they could, gnawing rope into threads,

chewing holes in nets that should never
have been cast; some get caught

in the space where *river* translates
into *ocean*; some make it out to the side

where the water is always bluer
only to learn that this side of the bay

is just a bigger net with smaller holes.
The only thing to do is to keep swimming.

Most go back at this point; their slick
oily skin isn't thick enough for all this salt.

The rest keep going, pushing through the tide,
befriending bigger fish with bigger teeth.

To My Future Sardines

And if one day

you find yourselves caught
in my net, it is not by accident.

I have long feared the fragility
of your minuscule bones but it is time I go fishing.

Do not swim away;

there are worse waters you could
find yourselves in. I am just salty

enough, just transparent enough;
I promise to be spacious enough.

I am one storm away

from extinction. As vast as I can be,
every river can run its course.

So I live by you, my heartbeat
the ripples from your caudal fins.

Acknowledgements

Firstly, a big thank you to Rebecca Kenny, for trusting my vision wholeheartedly and for being the biggest champion for marginalised voices. You're doing important work.

A massive thank you to the Manchester poetry community for welcoming me in with open arms and fully supporting my art.

All the gratitude to the lecturers in Creative Writing at The University of Bolton — in particular, Ben Wilkinson and Valerie O'Riordan, who have been incredibly supportive mentors, and instrumental in shaping the writer I am today.

And of course, thank you, dear reader, for picking up your rod and coming fishing with me. Sardines are slippery things, but we got there in the end. Your support means more than all of the oceans combined.

However, the biggest thank you, of course, goes to my family. My partner, Nat, for believing in me before I believed in myself. For coming along to that first open mic, and the one after, and the one after, and the one after, always cheering me on. Thank you for being my chief whooper.

To my mum, Anabela, thank you for always casting the net back out every time I swam away. Thank you for your unconditional love. This book is for you.

About the Author

Romina Ramos is a gender fluid Portuguese writer based in the North-West of England. Their writing explores themes of dislocation, identity, and intergenerational immigration. Their work has been shortlisted for the Penguin Random House imprint Merky Books New Writers' Prize and The Bridport Prize for Poetry; they also won the Carcanet Prize for Poetry.

They live in Bolton, with their partner, in an apartment that does not allow for plant keeping or pets, and sometimes smells likes Pizza Hut garlic bread. They brew coffee five days a week in order to pay for this luxury.

In February 2022, they started a new, inclusive open mic night, Natter, in the heart of Bolton with their pal Stuart Beveridge. It exists to create a platform for local creatives to share their work in a safe, supportive, and most importantly, free environment. You can check it out on Instagram, Twitter and TikTok at @NatterBolton.

About Bent Key

It started with a key.

Bent Key is named after the bent front-door key that Rebecca Kenny found in her pocket after arriving home from hospital following her car crash. It is a symbol — of change, new starts, risk, and taking a chance on the unknown.

Bent Key is a micropublisher with ethics. We do not charge for submissions, we do not charge to publish and we make space for writers who may struggle to access traditional publishing houses, specifically writers who are neuro-divergent or otherwise marginalised. We never ask anyone to write for free, and we like to champion authentic voices.

All of our beautiful covers are designed by our graphic designer Sam at SMASH Illustration, a graphic design company based in Southport, Merseyside.

Find us online:
bentkeypublishing.co.uk

Instagram & Facebook   @bentkeypublishing
Twitter   @bentkeypublish